ZOO ANIMAL
MYSTERIES

A Stickler
on Stilts

by Gillia M. Olson

Consulting Editor: Gail Saunders-Smith, PhD

Consultant: Jackie Gai, DVM
Zoo and Exotic Animal Consultant

CAPSTONE PRESS
a capstone imprint

Pebble Plus is published by Capstone Press,
151 Good Counsel Drive, P.O. Box 669, Mankato, Minnesota 56002.
www.capstonepub.com

032010
005740CGF10

 Books published by Capstone Press are manufactured with paper
containing at least 10 percent post-consumer waste.

Library of Congress Cataloging-in-Publication Data
Olson, Gillia M.
Stickler on stilts : a zoo animal mystery / by Gillia M. Olson.
p. cm.—(Pebble plus. Zoo animal mysteries)
Includes bibliographical references and index.
ISBN 978-1-4296-4500-3 (library binding)
1. Flamingos—Juvenile literature. I. Title. II. Series.
QL696.C56O47 2011
598.3'5—dc22   2010001346

Summary: Simple text and full-color photographs present a mystery zoo animal, one feature at a time, until its identity is revealed.

Editorial Credits
Jenny Marks, editor; Heidi Thompson, designer; Svetlana Zhurkin, media researcher; Eric Manske, production specialist

Photo Credits
Corbis/Bob Krist, 9, 11
iStockphoto/Brandon Laufenberg, cover
Nature Picture Library/Fabio Liverani, 7
Sarah Hatfield, 17
Shutterstock/Anna Omelchenko, 4–5; Carlos Caetano, 18–19; gary718, 20–21; Mashe, 14–15; Robbie Taylor, 13

Note to Parents and Teachers

The Zoo Animal Mysteries series supports science standards related to life science. This book
describes and illustrates flamingos. The images support early readers in understanding the
text. The repetition of words and phrases helps early readers learn new words. This book
also introduces early readers to subject-specific vocabulary words, which are defined in the
Glossary section. Early readers may need assistance to read some words and to use the Table of
Contents, Glossary, Read More, Internet Sites, and Index sections of the book.

Table of Contents

It's a Mystery

This book is full of clues
about a mystery zoo animal.
And the animal is me!
Can you guess what I am?

Here's your first clue:
In the wild, you'll find me
in salty lakes and lagoons.

North
America

Europe

Asia

Africa

South
America

Australia

Antarctica

■ **Where I Live**

5

My Life and Kids

I live in a big group with

thousands of others like me.

At night, we sometimes fly

to different spots to find food.

My mate and I build a tall nest.

We pile mud, small stones,

and feathers into a mound.

Our white egg sits on top.

9

Our baby has pink legs
and white feathers.
The feathers will change color
when our little bird grows up.

Body Parts

My hooked bill acts like a net.

Water passes through,

but food gets trapped.

I mostly eat tiny fish, insects,

crustaceans, and algae.

My long, skinny legs make it
easy to wade in the water.
I have wide, webbed feet
that keep me from sinking
in the mud.

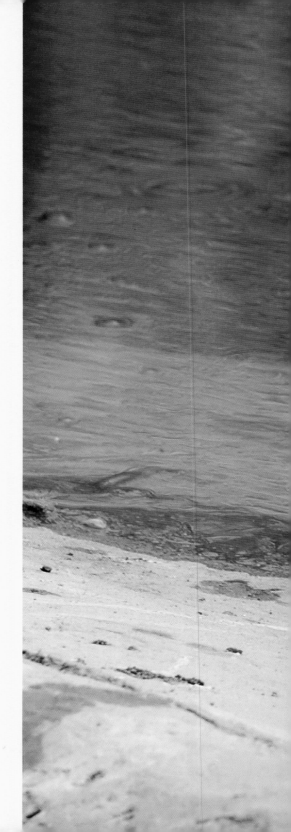

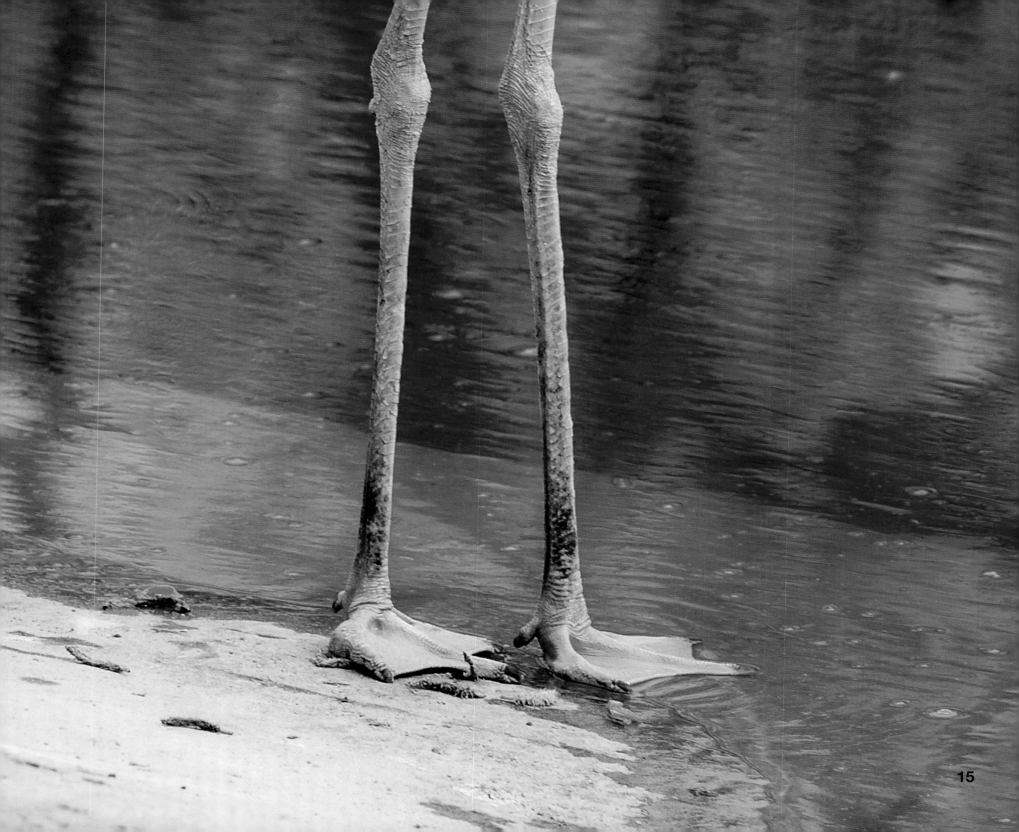

My yellow eyes see very well.

I have clear eyelids.

I can see when I blink!

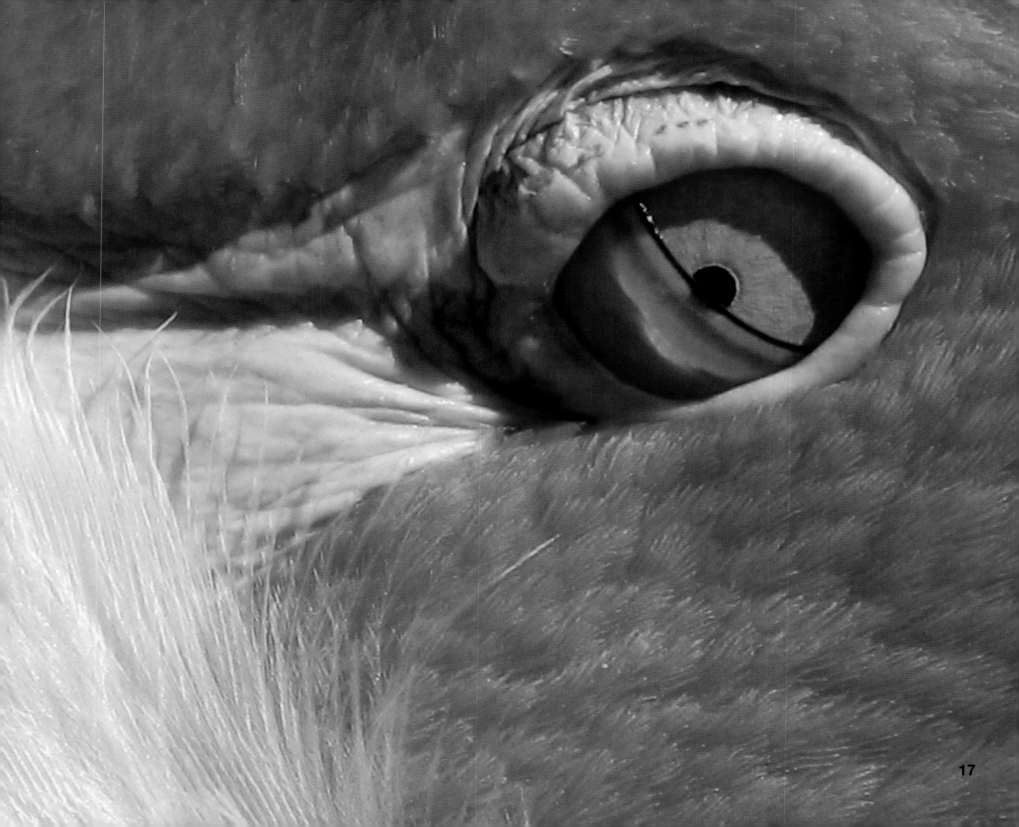

I'm best known

for my pink feathers.

The color comes from my food.

Have you guessed

what I am yet?

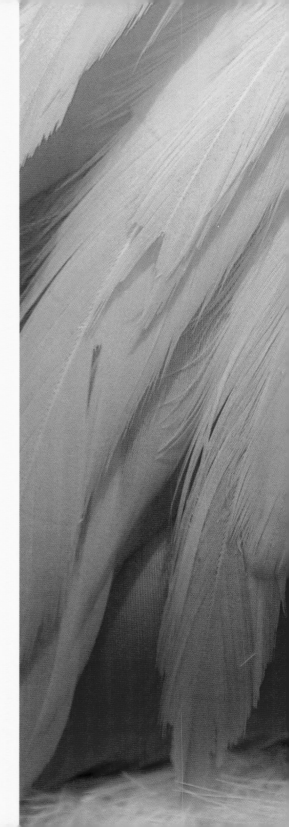

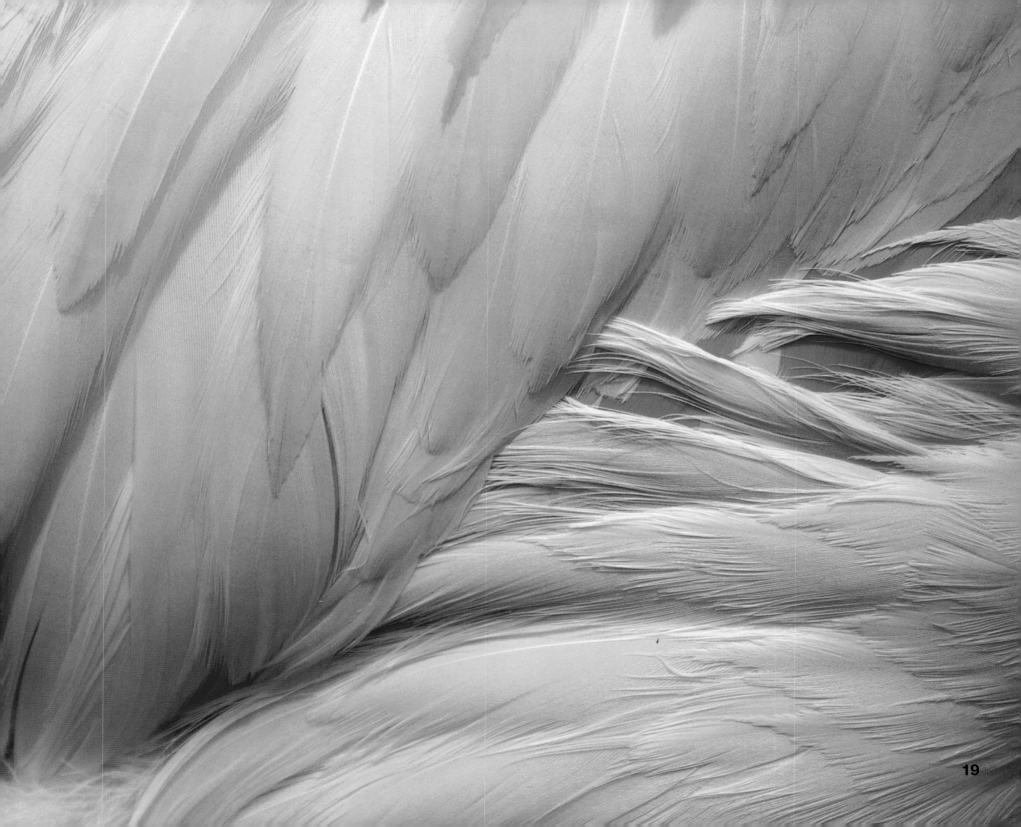

Mystery Solved!

I'm a flamingo!

This zoo mystery is solved.

Glossary

algae—small plants without roots or stems that grow in water

bill—the hard, pointed part of a bird's mouth

crustacean—an underwater animal with an outer skeleton, such as a lobster or shrimp

insect—a small animal with a hard outer shell, six legs, three body sections, and two antennas

lagoon—a shallow pool of seawater separated from the sea by a narrow strip of land

mate—one of a pair of animals

Read More

London, Jonathan. *Flamingo Sunset.* Tarrytown, N.Y.: Marshall Cavendish Children, 2008.

Macken, JoAnn Early. *The Life Cycle of a Flamingo.* Things with Wings. Milwaukee, Wis.: Weekly Reader Early Learning Library, 2006.

Malone, Jean M. *Flamingos.* All Aboard Science Reading. New York: Grosset and Dunlap, 2009.

Internet Sites

FactHound offers a safe, fun way to find Internet sites related to this book. All of the sites on FactHound have been researched by our staff.

Here's all you do:

Visit *www.facthound.com*

Type in this code: 9781429645003

Index

Word Count: 195
Grade: 1
Early-Intervention Level: 15